On A More Serious Note

On A More Serious Note

Poems: a coffee cream collection,
both light and dark.

J. B. EDEN

AuthorHouse™
1663 Liberty Drive
Bloomington, IN 47403
www.authorhouse.com
Phone: 1-800-839-8640

© *2013 by J. B. Eden. All rights reserved.*

No part of this book may be reproduced, stored in a retrieval system, or transmitted by any means without the written permission of the author.

Published by AuthorHouse   04/20/2013

ISBN: 978-1-4817-9060-4 (sc)
ISBN: 978-1-4817-9061-1 (e)

Any people depicted in stock imagery provided by Thinkstock are models, and such images are being used for illustrative purposes only.
Certain stock imagery © Thinkstock.

This book is printed on acid-free paper.

Because of the dynamic nature of the Internet, any web addresses or links contained in this book may have changed since publication and may no longer be valid. The views expressed in this work are solely those of the author and do not necessarily reflect the views of the publisher, and the publisher hereby disclaims any responsibility for them.

This book is dedicated to Shelley, Nicola and Richard.
With thanks for many happy memories.

Contents

Lighter Moments
Listen, Look, Touch And Dream 2
Busy All Day Long 4
Snap-shots of England 5
Aqua-splash! 6
What can I tell you? 8
The Moon 9
The South Downs 10
We're British! 11
The River 12
Midsummer? 13
I Remember 14
The Ways of the Sea 16
Shades Of Autumn 17
The Chocolate Cake 18
Is It Spring? 19
Happy Thoughts 20
Freedom 21
Should Poems Rhyme? 22

Darker Notes
D(ie)rama 25
2003–The Disputed War 26
The Meteorite 27
A Mighty Fall 28
1914-18 29
A Promise Of Summer 30
The Reckoning 31
Where Are We Going? 32

The In-between Years 33
All In The Mind..34
An Earthly Hell...35
Urban Wild Life..36
A New Millennium 37
And Tomorrow?..38
A Modern Life..40
Suburbia..41
Inside Out..42
The Final Curtain 43

Happy Endings
A Night Out...47
Sunrise 48
At The Beach..49
Dog Grooming..50
Ski Scare..51
The Family Fruit Cake 52
The Weekly Shop..53
Mottisfont Abbey..54
Sea and Sand 55
The Wanderer 56
Chelsea..57
June Nights..58
The Early Bird..60
The End Of The Day...61
Sunset On The Isle Of Mull..62

Lighter Moments

Listen, Look, Touch And Dream
A celebration of the sea.

Listen!
The sea is near.
What can you hear?
Whispering and splashing,
Pattering and crashing.
Now the waves sigh
And the seagulls cry.

Look!
See, the tide courses.
Watch the white horses
Dipping and diving,
Hardly surviving!
Enjoying their ride,
Then gone with the tide.

Touch!
As the shadows steal
What can you feel?
The cold tingle of spray
As the waves rush away.
The soft, creamy foam,
Before you go home.

Dream!
Of gentle sea motion:
Relaxing potion.
Pretend you're afloat
In a cushion lined boat
And be lulled to sleep
By the sea.

Busy All Day Long

Things to do, things to do.
Now, where's my list, not one but two!
Clothes to wash, bulbs to plant,
Dinner to cook; no wait – I can't.
Have to shop first, stock up with food.
Yes, I know we have tins, no need to be rude!
Back with supplies, enough for a siege.
Some for the cupboard, some to freeze.
I'm halfway down list number one.
Time for coffee, another job done.

Now veg to peel, meat to brown,
Put on hold that trip to town.
The ironing can wait,
The windows, too.
Let's sit and chat
Just me and you!

Snap-shots of England

Sun shines, rain falls;
Rainbows come and go.
Frost glistens, clouds gather—here comes the snow.
The weather is a talking point with everyone I know!
The colour of our nation depends from first to last
Upon the BBC and its weather forecast.
Cities can be grey,
Or mellow yellow stone
Hewed from distant quarries, where honey bees drone.

The countryside is different with brown and green and gold;
And multi-coloured flowers, a joy to behold.
Through all the changing seasons the colours come and go;
In suburbs, towns and villages,
The England that I know.
There is a sense of purpose, and nature lends a hand,
So join the celebration of our green and pleasant land!

Aqua-splash!
(By request for the Meon Valley Aqua-fitters)

On Tuesday morn the members arrive,
Whatever the weather, along they drive.
They gather to chatter and splash.

Each one signs in at the leisure club desk
And hurries off to change.
The men turn left and the ladies right,
Then they all re-appear in gear quite
    strange,
A truly awesome sight!
The late-comer enters now with a dash
Attracting some comical looks.
They gather to chatter and splash.

"Right," calls out their instructor,
"No slacking for today.
We're being filmed for this new course.
Stay in your lines, don't stray!"

They jog in time, then sideways run
And really try so hard,
But the one at the back is miles away;
On her holiday in Liskeard:
She was still on 'spotty dog'
When the others 'skied' then swam
And now there's a mighty collision
With a frightful traffic jam!

"Oh heavens above!" a shrill voice cries.
"You've spoiled my film debut!"
But the class had dissolved into giggling
    asides
At the luckily painless to-do.
The pattern had gone, the rhythm was
    lost,
All eyes were on the crash.
"That's it for today, we'll do it next week,
When you gather to chatter and splash!"

What can I tell you?

What can I tell you baby, bright eyes so clear?
What things would I want you to hear?

I can tell you of sights, so amazing and strange
In wonderful lands far away.
Of cultures so different from yours and mine
That you may come across one day.
I want you to learn of the worthwhile things
That interest, excite and inspire:
Have the knowledge and colour and confidence
That your brand new life will require.

The Moon

Earth's mystical, magical moon,
Pale and serene in the night sky
Hiding its mountainous landscape
From the human eyes that pry.

How brightly the moonlight shines
Down from the cool, yellow globe;
While twinkling all round are the stars,
Designs on a blue velvet robe.

The moon remains steadfast and true
In a sky that changes and seems
To trick us with weatherly foibles;
Yet still the patient moon beams.

The South Downs

The rolling South Downs are balm
to the soul.
The views are quite stunning,
green and gold;
They roll on and on for miles and
then more,
Soft, grassy meadows and sheep galore.

In quiet contemplation the rat race
slows down,
Peace reigns, just enjoy, forget the town.
Stroll on Devil's Dyke: take a picnic
to share,
Do something you like,
Sing and dance if you dare!

Let the stress of the week evaporate,
Embrace nature's gift:
Let tomorrow's cares wait.

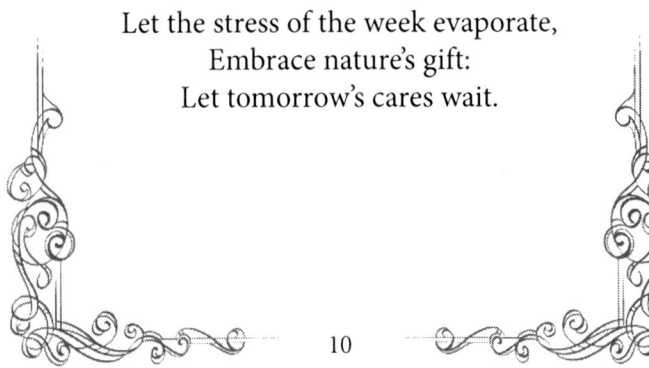

We're British!

How patiently we stand in orderly queues.
There's something rather grand, in ones,
 in twos.
We never push and shove, never try to
 cheat
Whatever the weather, in sun, snow or
 sleet;
But with aching feet wait
For the bus that's often late.

We queue to buy goods, too,
And rarely hear complaints.
The palace guards stand ramrod straight
Until the odd one faints
When the sun beats down
From a sky clear and blue.
Whatever the weather, whatever the
 place,
We're British so we queue!

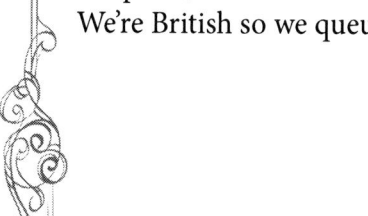

The River

The river meanders through a beautiful
   valley.
There are blossoms that perfume the air;
Wonderfully twisted shapes line its banks.
Butterflies settle, free from care.
The whole of the valley is happy.
It shimmers in the sun, sighing with
   contentment
As the river flows on.

Slowly it gathers pace, growing more
   powerful.
Each watery surge adds momentum until,
Round the next sharp-angled bend
A sudden rush, then spumes of spray –
Rocks in the way, a weir!
Our river catches its breath as it falls,
Bright drops pierce the air.
Still exhilarating from its descent
It rounds the next bend.
Then, flowing more gently
The river meanders through a beautiful
   valley.

Midsummer?

It seems as though the summer has arrived
With long, hot days and really sticky nights;
And memories of camping trips survived
Come back to whet our outdoor appetites.

Those lazy days spent gazing out to sea;
Make sure the children stay within the bounds!
Then ambling back to base in time for tea
And listening to the different seaside sounds.

Out comes the suntan lotion once again,
The cotton tops and straw hats re-appear.
That extra weight of winter is a pain;
Those shorts will never button up this year!

But tomorrow will be winter wear, they say,
As torrential rain and thunder rule the day.

I Remember
(Written for a competition celebrating
Thomas Hood)

I remember, I remember
The train that took me there.
It groaned and creaked despairingly,
It made me stop and stare.
It shunted in so slowly
And shuddered to a halt;
Hissing, sighing, gasping,
A sudden final jolt.

I remember, I remember
The sultry, humid heat.
Eleven at night and oh, so dark
When we clambered to our feet
From the ancient Ambassador taxi
Into the pitch black night.
Jhunjhunu station car park—
Ahead and to the right.

I remember, I remember
Finally climbing inside.
No seats but shelves for sleeping on!
My courage waned and died.
How narrow the space, how claustrophobic;
Mine was the middle of three.
"I really can't get into there—."
"Oh, yes you can, you'll see!"

I remember, I remember
A journey, and well I may,
From the midnight desert of Rajasthan
To a city far away.
A long, hot journey of wonderful things.
Could it have been a dream?
But then the daylight filtered through
And Delhi could be seen!

The Ways of the Sea

The sea has many faces
And individual traits:
Different moods in different places,
And it comes to him who waits.
But for those who are impatient,
Yearning to be free,
The sea provides a highway,
Escape for you and me!

The sea provides the answer
To many of our needs.
It nurtures diverse sealife
And wonderful seaweeds.
The sea will bring things to us
Yet also take away.
It can be kind; it can be cruel;
So different every day.

From a crashing, roaring monster
Intent on breaking through
Whatever things obstruct it,
Manmade and natural, too,
The sea can change so quickly
To a restful, shimmering scene,
To soothe and bring us comfort,
A prop on which to lean.

Shades Of Autumn

The man of the house is busy
And has been all day long.
He's tidying up the garden
With lopper, spade and prong.
The autumn leaves are many,
They cover everything,
But our gardening man is happy there,
I think I hear him sing!

Half way through this busy day
He'll take a little break;
Come in for tea and biscuits
Prop up the fork and rake,
And put away the spade,
Stand the lopper by the door
Then leave great muddy footprints
Across the kitchen floor!

The Chocolate Cake

It looked so delicious
In its chocolate overcoat;
The sugary decorations
Brought a lump to the throat.
There were flowers in bunches
They really were delightful –
Much too good to eat,
But the calories were frightful.
It said on the box
Three hundred per slice.
In fact it was repeated
Not once but twice.
Alas, it didn't say
How big that slice could be:
Perhaps the cake served ten
And not just three!

Is It Spring?

Hey, look! There's a patch of blue sky.
It's been a long time coming.
There's a break in the grey, cloud covered
 dome
And a glimmer of yellow up high.

Wait, stop! Maybe its too soon
To cast off winter clothes.
But for a while we'll bask in the weak
 little rays
Shining down through the wintry gloom.

Happy Thoughts

Let's all have a giggle,
Its good for the soul.
It can be contagious
And catch those nearby:
So find something funny,
No need to cry.

More muscles are needed
To smile than to frown;
Face life with a big grin,
Try not to feel down.

Let's laugh and be happy,
Its good for our health.
It brightens our life,
Sends problems away.
So think merry thoughts
And have a good day!

Freedom

Floating weightless,
Rising on a gentle tide,
Ever moving, ever swelling,
Build up high and then subside.

Make your choice and choose with care
For freedom isn't everywhere.

Should Poems Rhyme?
A matter of opinion

We've had this argument before
And I maintain my view;
You think a poem needn't rhyme,
But I absolutely do!

Darker Notes

D(ie)rama
Ode to a beautiful plant

They hung,

The beautiful bells.

A graceful arch of magenta

From a slender slope of green;

Gently swaying in a summer breeze;

Dancing, playing, never still; enhancing, entrancing until

The storm struck with vengeful force:
Bolt of lightning, crash of thunder.
Harmed by hailstones, torn asunder
The beautiful bells,

They
Fell.

2003 – The Disputed War

While the politicians talk, the
soldiers walk
Towards their uncertain future.
While helicopters throb
Families sob,
Left behind to wonder.
You can hear the sceptics shout:
What's it all about?

Just how did this chaos start?
Will it tear MPs apart?
The rallying cry is absent; there is no firm
agreement.
This time they'll follow where another
will lead.
Of the masses – take no heed!
Why listen to the nation?
What – include participation?

And so
We, and the world, await the long-term
outcome
With fear and trepidation.

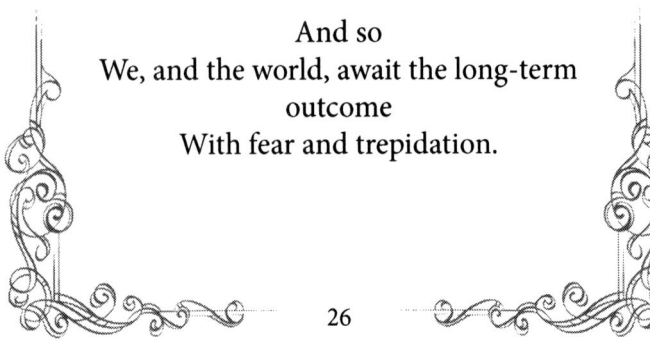

The Meteorite
(February 15th 2013)

It streaked across the sky,
In the twinkling of an eye,
A shining light,
A blazing trail, burning bright.
And those below looked with delight.

Then – havoc as it split asunder
A huge explosion, dreadful thunder.

Glass was shattered, buildings shook
A moment here, that's all it took.
Now people looked with trepidation
A meteorite had come to earth
With pain and devastation.

A Mighty Fall

The wind blew powerfully and down
    came the tree.
It had been there for many a year.
"Look," said the neighbours, who came
    round to see,
And some even shed a quiet tear,
"We've lost all that shade and such beauty,
    too."
They glanced around at the elm and the
    oak,
There was also a large spreading yew.
But the tree so loved by the village folk
That had guarded the scene for so long
Was the one by the green that cut such a
    dash,
The fall that was greeted with sadness,
    alas,
Was a beautiful old English ash.

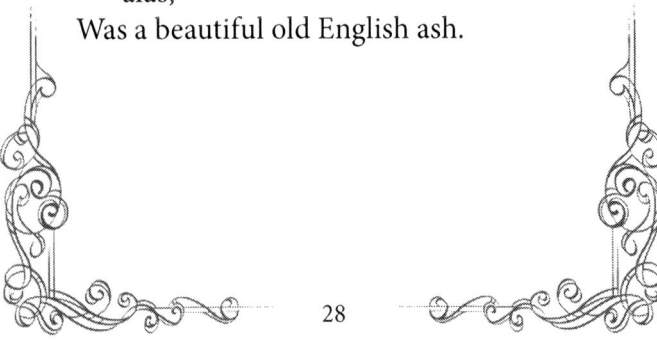

1914 -18

The marching feet plod wearily on,
A long way still to go.
Their marching orders came at dawn
When sleet had turned to snow.
With empty stomachs and little hope
The men marched on in fear:
They faced starvation and weather so
    cold,
A dreadful end to the year.
And when at last they stopped to rest,
The trenches now in sight,
Those weary men with frightened souls
Found strength enough to fight.
They rested in the muddy pits
Before the final cry;
Then heaved their bodies, as of one,
Over the top to die.

A Promise Of Summer

This year the season started very well,
In May the sun was shining every day;
The sky was azure blue and no rain fell.
New plants produced a beautiful display
When carefully placed in the fresh-dug ground.
The frogs were hopping all around the pond
Where evidence of mating could be found!

The early morning birdsong filled the air
And blackbirds pecked for worms amongst the dew.
The garden warblers sang without a care
And filled our hearts with promises anew.
Just then we heard a clap of distant thunder
And heavy showers of cold, torrential rain
Came down to tear our summer days asunder.

The Reckoning

I feel it in my bones.
Its creeping nearer,
All the way.

I hear it in the trees,
Its sounding clearer
Day by day.

I feel it all around me,
Its in the very air;
Here to stay
Come what may,
Day by judgement day.

I wonder how I'll feel,
What will there be,
Some kind of beckoning?
Will it seem real,
This final day of reckoning?

Where Are We Going?

Jam-packed roads and crowded trains,
Dozens of buses too full to stop.
Everyone hurrying, no-one gains.
Where are we going?
Why do we rush till we drop?

A compulsion, a pushing, a lemming like
  instinct?
What makes us behave like scurrying
  ants,
Too busy to take a deep breath:
Have we lost the perception to linger and
  wonder,
To slow down the pace and remember the
  pleasures?
So, just for a moment – STOP!
Stop right where you are, look around,
  take stock.
Or, now for a minute consider the
  measures
By which you plan your clock.
Let your mind drift away, leave the cares
  of the day,
Before you continue your frantic trip,
That endless trip to – nowhere.

The In-between Years

Where has the in-between gone?

From thirty to sixty
In the twinkling of an eye
The years disappeared
Like the breath of a sigh.
So much has occurred
And important things, too.
Yet, like the flight of a bird
The years slipped through.

Just how has the in-between gone?
To leave us alone
In a twilight zone,
The fading notes of a song.

All In The Mind

How strange the things that enter one's mind
Unbidden, not thought of, but suddenly there.
What prompts them to come uninvited, unkind?
Stirring up memories with feelings laid bare.

The brain is amazing and still quite unknown
In its depths of behaviour and traits:
Quite a small mass of grey matter and bone.
And the rest of the body awaits
While the complex machine is whirring away
Sending out messages both night and day,

The human computer works throughout life
With so many facets at play:
It copes with happiness, trouble and strife:
Relax, let your mind have its say.

An Earthly Hell
(After reading a depressing novel)

We freeze all night, and sweat all day
And nothing takes the pain away.
We smash the rocks and split the stones,
No-one hears our cries and moans.

We're building roads from here to there;
No names given, we don't care.

If we had food, a good night's sleep
Then maybe we could smile, not weep.
Another blizzard, ice and snow:
A few more dead and more to go.

A wrong word here, a gesture there
Condemned to a life we cannot bear.
These were our crimes, if crimes they be,
So innocent for all to see.
When will mankind change wicked ways?
Till then I'll simply count the days
With fellow women roped together,
Support ourselves through ghastly
    weather.
Hoping to live till freedom day
Keeping death at bay.

Urban Wild Life

The urban fox has learnt new ways,
He forages in pastures new.
No fields for him, but tarmac roads
And living prey is far and few.
He rummages in bags and bins
For any scraps of likely food.
The urban fox is now so tame
And hunts in such a different mood.
If you leave shoes outside your door
Or gardening gloves up on the wall,
He'll wander by quite casually
And calmly steal them all!

The urban fox is here to stay
So guard your treasures, night and day.

A New Millennium
(Approaching 2000)

Momentous! Memorable? Millennium mayhem.
Slipping relentlessly nearer, closer day by day.
Look how the fever is spreading,
Gripping new patients with fervour,
Loosening their grip on reality,
In the melange of ideas at play.
How to celebrate? What to build? When to advertise
Their new inventions, quite fantastic, all will have their say.
Too big, too small, too high, too tall! Shall we sympathize?
Can we hope for common sense to intervene at last;
To curb the wild excesses and introduce some calm;
To slow the race for changes and consider what has passed,
Take on board a history lesson
Before the die is cast?

And Tomorrow?

It started with a very unusual sky;
That May day.
The clouds were banked high, really high
　in the sky
On that day.

"Look", said the children, on their way to
　school,
"Look up there".
They stared with dismay, "Will it rain on
　our play?"
Not THIS day.

The milkman finished his morning
　round.
The float stopped.
He sighed and stepped out; there was
　no-one about
At that time.

He scratched his head and looked
　puzzled.
Why so dark?
A postman appeared, "Hey, look, ain't
　that weird?
What a day!"

The men stood side by side, wondering.
On that grim day.
The clouds were now an ominous green,
Lit by something as yet unseen.
On that day.

Now everyone, everywhere, stopped in their tracks,
Staring skywards.
While the green rolling mist approached with a twist
Enveloping all in its way,
That strange day.

And the planet we used to call Earth
Featured no more in the universe
That weird day.
But freedom was found in the misty surround
On that day.
And everyone sang in unison with one united voice.
Just once.
And there echoed around a wonderful sound,
That last day.

A Modern Life
(From a Senior's view!)

Why is everything so complicated?
Is nothing simple anymore?
We do our best and try so hard
To open technologies coded door.

A remote for this, a remote for that;
No need to move, just sit and get fat!
So many buttons to press with a finger;
Life in fast forward, no time to linger.

There are many advances
And programmes galore
With technical help –
Its out there for sure.
The drawback is,
And it seems so sad,
Today's technology
DRIVES US MAD.

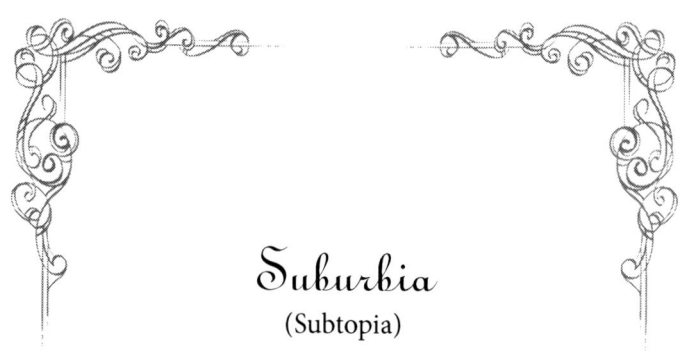

Suburbia
(Subtopia)

Neither here nor there, but always
    in-between
The busy, throbbing city and the
    countryside so green.
Just when were they invented?
How did they come to be
Just between the country and the city or
    the sea?

Rows and rows of boxes, lining avenues;
Houses, bungalows and flats with no
    good views.
Intermittent bus stops, a school, some
    swings, a shop.
Maybe a little shrubbery where dog
    walkers can stop.

But they're all so very soul-less.
Do the planners care
About those in-betweeny suburbs
That are neither here nor there?

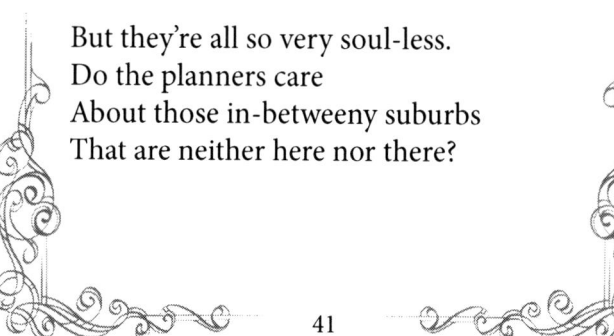

Inside Out

I smile at the birds as they soar and glide
So effortless, light and free.
As they wing through the air
I smile with my friends,
But I'm silently crying inside.

I stand by the sea and watch the tide
As it gently ebbs and flows;
A sense of peace and tranquillity,
But I'm jumbled up inside.

In practical terms there's a great divide
With the human race as a whole.
So much injustice and misery
And I wish I felt better inside.

The Final Curtain

(A story in 50 words)

The lights went out.

Action; music; song; dance!
Applause.
They strolled home giggling.
She opened the door.
He sniffed – gas?
She reached for the light switch.
"No!" he shouted.
A spark, a flash.
They staggered blindly.
Life floated by; hung suspended, then fell.
All action ceased.

Their lights went out.

Happy Endings

A Night Out

The curtain rises slowly,
The lights becoming low,
Anticipation all around;
We're ready for the show.

With actors in the wings
And scenery in place
We want to see the hero
In this dramatic race.

We do not know the story
But wait with baited breath
To witness what will follow,
Will there be another death?

At last the play is over.
The atmosphere was fraught;
Once again the hero triumphed
And the villains all were caught!

Sunrise

A clear night sky brings a hint of frost:
The sunset colours lost.
But when morning dawns with the
    rising sun
A new palette has begun.
Such brilliant reds light up the day
And glorious colours show the way
Till the rising sun, a yellow ball,
Shines over the land to cheer us all.

At The Beach

Waves crash,
Water rises,
Shingle rattles,
In for surprises.
Shells washed up
Then dragged away.
Seabirds dive-
They're coming our way!

Boats out sailing
Riding the swell:
Icecream cart
Sounding its bell.
Children paddle
While adults survey
The busy scene
All round the bay.

Seaside,
Happy days:
Long, hot summer,
Lazy ways.
Children splashing,
Tingling cheeks,
Building castles,
Wonderful weeks!

Dog Grooming

They come in every month or two
For their essential grooming;
Washed and dried, with nails cut short,
They have their owners swooning!
Such handsome beasts when trimmed
    and toned,
You'll never see one better.
From top to tail, each hair in place
Chihuahua or Red Setter.

The Poodle causes problems, though,
Its body closely shaved:
A pompom here, a pompom there
And dignity is saved!

Ski Scare

The lift to carry them to the top stopped.
Now what was wrong?
It should go on.
They were well and truly stuck – not
    down, not up.
Although the view was really great
It certainly didn't compensate
For the thrill of the speed downhill,
The whoosh of skis,
The icy cold breeze,
Zigzag, miss those trees!

A movement at last, the danger's passed.
They travel on up to the snowy peaks,
Jump off the lift with nervous shrieks.
Then weaving and bobbing
Race down the run;
This is the life, so much fun.

Back to the village just in time
For a nice hot bath and a glass of wine.

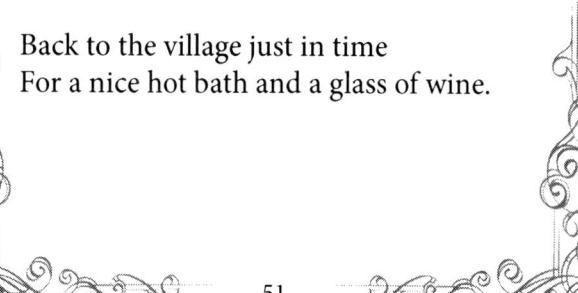

The Family Fruit Cake
(The edible one!)

For this you need to be prepared.
Sultanas, sugar, nothing spared,
With eggs and flour and butter, too,
To make this cake for me and you.
Add orange zest, with juice and spice
These give a lift that's really nice.
Mix together with a good, strong beat.
Now bring the oven up to heat.
Don't forget to grease the tin;
Carefully pour the mixture in
And bake for just an hour or more.
Children line up at the kitchen door,
Wonderful smells to tempt taste buds,
But first, washing up with lots of suds!

Now for the best bit – a tasting for all,
With plates held out, careful, don't fall!
Gathered around the still warm bake
The chatter subsides while they munch
   the cake.

The Weekly Shop
On the hill near my home.

Funny little man
In your baggy shorts,
Looking rather hassled
And very out of sorts.
Stopping for a deep breath
While puffing up the hill,
Then picking up the bags again
And summoning the will,
Command the aching legs
To make the final climb
Into the pretty garden
With the view sublime.
Time for tea and biscuits,
The mission is complete;
Collapse on the sofa,
Put up your feet!

Mottisfont Abbey

The heavenly scent of roses galore
Filled the air;
And all around the people strolled
Here a group, there a pair,
Admiring the garden and sharing
    thoughts.

Mottisfont Abbey at its best,
The lovely gardens newly dressed.

Then into the House to view the art.
So much to see!
Look all around, where to go?
A plan to follow, just wander, feel free.
We peer into rooms where the famous
    have stood.

Now to a place with a secret to share.
The Whistler room.
It truly is a sight to behold,
With elegant drapes and trompe-l'œil
    quite rare
And a history waiting to be told.

A quiet wander back by the River Test
Viewing the Font on the way.
We'll leave the garden and House to rest
At the end of a lovely day.

Sea and Sand

Hooray for school holidays!

The children came running with buckets
    and spades,
While the adults plodded behind,
Laden with mats and balls and bats,
Not to mention the picnic and chairs.

They scrambled and clambered over the
    dunes
And finally found a space
To set up a camp at last, thank God!
And put down their heavy loads.

Now the adults could rest, drink tea and
    chat,
Exchange the news of the day.
Gaze out at the swimmers and fishing
    boats
While the children started to play.

The Wanderer

He saw high mountains topped with snow,
Where the Yeti was said to have trod.
He gazed from a distance at smoking volcanoes
Where no human being could go.
He followed his dream.

There were rivers that rushed over rock,
Tumbling down to the sea,
No ripples there but a torrent wild.
He stood here in awe to take stock.
He followed his dream.

He struggled through jungles and harsh terrain,
Meeting the challenges there.
Living with tribes in makeshift camps;
Listening, then telling his story again.
Forever maintaining his dream.

Now he no longer needs to roam:
Has memories to treasure forever.
So many places and wonderful sights,
Time to head for home.
He truly had followed his dream.

Chelsea

There was a buzz of excitement!
The weather was fine.
Along the Embankment, around Sloane
   Square
Were hundreds of people;
A long snaky line.

There were lots of policemen
And helpers as well.
Red-coated pensioners wandered about,
Glad to be part of the scene,
Part of the human swell.

There was so much to look at,
Such magic to see:
All the shapes and the colours
Of this year's Chelsea!
There were wonderful images,
Fragrant perfumes:
Intricate patterns and delicate blooms.
In all their glory
The fruits and the flowers,
In pots and vases and beautiful bowers.

A day was too short to take it all in.
Three acres of marquee alone!
But we saw what we could,
And there's one thing I know . . . .
We shall treasure the memories
Of Chelsea Flower Show.

June Nights

The month of June has arrived at last,
Long-awaited with impatience.
Now winter seems a world away
And there we hope it will stay!
The day is over;
Now follows a night of comfortable
    darkness,
Heady perfumes
And warm, warm air to caress bare arms
And cherish the soul.

Perched on the edge of a raised flower
    bed
Holding a glass of wine,
Enveloped in the scent from the
    Zepherine Drouin,
No thorns but a wonderful bloom.
Listen, the distant low drone of an
    aircraft,
Pinpricks of light but no shape.
Then the plop of a frog as it hops in the
    pond
And the patter of foxes' feet.

The sky seems made of velvet
With the moon appliquéd on,
And a million stars, like sequins,
Shimmer and sparkle, firing the night.
Look! There's a moth: so silent
Just a glimmer of wings as it brushes by.
Now the glass is empty;
Time to take a deep breath, intoxicating
    air.
Sleep well, sleep deep, dream happily.
June nights are here for a while.

The Early Bird
A Premature Event

He wouldn't wait for two more months,
Impatient to see the light.
He sprung his surprise in the early hours,
On a cold, dark winter night:
And when dawn came he glimpsed
a world
Of comfort, warmth and calm.
An incubator ready and bright
To keep him safe from harm.
A tiny wee body in sleep so sound
So perfect yet so small,
A little round face and skin so soft,
He wriggled and charmed us all.
Delicate fingers, minute toes,
Such clear blue eyes
And a button nose!
With a woolly hat upon his head
He'll soon be home in his own bed.

The End Of The Day

The sun is setting now
The colours seem untrue,
Bright oranges and pinks
With the last few streaks of blue.
I can see some tiny stars
Beginning to shine anew;
Twinkling and fading
Against the deepening blue.
It won't be very long before
The sounds of night come through
To add to the picture
Against the midnight blue.

Sunset On The Isle Of Mull
Easter 2013

Apricot, lavender and pale, pale pinks
With just a hint of blue.
Long thin shadows and fading light;
Distant hills with orange hue.
A deepening red creeps over the land,
Creating a wonderful view.

Across the loch, now colour striped,
The mountains, topped with snow,
Have bands of pink and orange
A dramatic evening show!
From coast to coast across the isle
Mull now is all aglow.

Lightning Source UK Ltd.
Milton Keynes UK
UKOW040353220513

211059UK00001B/14/P